P^{THE}ROFICIENT MANAGER

P THE ROFICIENT MANAGER

Simple Practical Advice and Tips for Becoming a 21st Century Proficient Manager

GAURAV GULATI

PARTRIDGE
A Penguin Random House Company

To order additional copies of this book, contact
Partridge India
000 800 10062 62
orders.india@partridgepublishing.com

www.partridgepublishing.com/india

CONTENTS

DEDICATION

This book is dedicated to my parents, my wife and everyone who is passionate about management and leadership.

In Honor of

My Father,

All my teachers and

Bristol Business School-University of the West of England

In Memory of

My late grandparents Mr. Hans Raj Gulati & Mrs. Raj Kumari Gulati and late maternal grandmother

Proficient Manager
I N S T I T U T E

Our Mission is Creating Knowledge and Developing Ethical Proficient Managers and Leaders for a Global Society.

The Proficient Manager Institute is an International professional body formed for the purpose of providing professionals and managers with the opportunity to be proficient manager and proficient leader. We are devoted in providing the most practical and useful information around the world to improve the way people handle their work, team, clients, projects, requirements through innovative learning.

In today's competitive environment manager's work in an age of continuous change, organizations today require Proficient Managers and Leaders who can address demanding challenges and have the ability to develop and implement the most effective business strategies to solve these problems.

Our core purpose is to develop the key skills required for efficient management. Through our certification and qualifying system we strive to build knowledge and understanding of management and leadership skills so that our qualified proficient managers have the necessary skills to improve their performance and to enable them to have a rewarding career in management.

For more information about Proficient Manager Institute visit: www.proficientmanager.com or Email: info@proficientmanager.com

ABOUT THE AUTHOR

Gaurav Gulati is the founder of Proficient Manager Institute, an international professional body formed for empowering managers. He is a management consultant & coach and has experience working with multinational corporations as an employee, consultant and coach.

Gaurav is a Certified Six Sigma Black Belt Professional & PMP. He holds a Master of Business Administration in Marketing, PGD in International Management from University of the West of England, Bristol, UK and a Bachelor in Business Administration & Hotel Management from Allahabad Agricultural Institute (now Sam Higginbottom Institute of Agriculture, Technology and Sciences).

As a coach, he is a highly effective professional coach with a track record of success in assisting top management, managers and experienced professionals to make personal transformations relating to interpersonal skills, mindfulness, emotional intelligence and personal fulfillment. Along with this he also delivers guest lectures on management and leadership at colleges and universities.

As a management consultant, Gaurav has advised and worked closely with top management. He has turned around failing business performance of many companies and he specializes in supporting entrepreneurial growth businesses transition to a more disciplined approach to management.

His consulting services include organizational design, strategic, operational and financial planning, business process improvement, executive training, leadership assessment and business development. He combines his solid business acumen with the best coaching models to support the delivery of sustainable solutions to his clients.

Prior to his work as management consultant and coach, he worked in United Kingdom and India as a corporate executive and manager in Hospitality, Insurance, Information Technology and E-commerce sector.

For more information about Gaurav Gulati, please visit: www.gauravgulati.com or Email: info@gauravgulati.com

PREFACE

In this competitive world the corporate pressures, stress, work load and multitasking has kind of intricate our life, therefore it has become essential to learn how to handle responsibilities and manage various activities perfectly and smoothly.

This book will attempt to put you on path of essential change so you may become proficient manager and get real respect and honor you deserve being executive, manager, professional or entrepreneur.

What Kind of Book is this?

The Proficient Manager is an essential change path that aims to introduce you to values, discipline, management and leadership practices that should be followed by every manager to become proficient manager.

This book is different as it does not focus on technical and academic proficiency but features skills and qualities that focus on human side of management as proficiency is not just limited to analytical and technical skills only. The Proficient Manager is packed with ideas, tips and stories to offer quick and practical advice on how to manage yourself, your team, customers and your organization.

Who Should Read This Book

Anybody interested in management and leadership can read this book as it aims to enlighten you with knowledge to enhance your managerial skills and understanding.

How to Read This Book

This book will help you elucidate the problems that distress us every day; you will find simple solutions to common problems. It is meant for all nature of professionals willing to manage everything smoothly and systematically along with the need to balance work, family, and career building.

Don't be in hurry while reading this book, try to apply what you learn, share, and discuss with your close once as doing so will surely enhance your understanding and skills better.

ACKNOWLEDGEMENTS

Writing book and effort to match expectations of self and others is not the simple job; to produce a meaningful and worthy book requires lot of co-operation, assistance and ideas from other people.

I would like to thank my father Mr. Ripu Daman Gulati, my mother Mrs. Kamini Gulati and wife Ritika Gulati, whose patience and support was really helpful in writing this book.

I would also like to thank all the professionals from worldwide who participated in various surveys conducted by me and have made this publication possible.

Many stats, facts, quotes, stories and examples have been taken from various sources like blogs, newspapers, magazines, books and websites. I have tried my best to mention all the sources but in case any source is not mention as source is anonymous, I would like to express my gratitude to everyone whose work has contributed to this book.

Brief History of Management

Ancient Empires and Emperors:

Though it is really difficult to tell when exactly the management practices and leadership started in the history but we can accept as true that it existed in history. Formation of different civilizations and story of great emperors prove that both management and leadership always existed. Not getting into the depth of history with examples of Indus Valley civilization, Roman Civilization etc and applying common sense we can understand that is not possible for a common person to lead thousands and millions of soldiers as its followers without having leadership qualities. Leaders could be good or bad with good or bad leadership styles but it is true that the emperors were definitely the leaders. Along with this I would also like to mention that the ways the great emperors handle their empires with help of their ministers and soldier is a good example of management. Emperor work was not just expanding their empires and fighting wars but they also had to manage and maintain their empires and generate revenue from different forms of duties and taxes.

Industrial Revolution and Post Industrial Revolution:

The Industrial Revolution is the biggest turning point in history, this phase changed the way of life as it developed two classes in society that was employees and employers. Industrial Revolution is the point when development of management theories and practices took place and Post-Industrial Revolution is the point when employers first realized that without correct management practices and leadership it is not possible to identify, develop, retain and make the most out of their high potential employees. Great Scholars like Fredrick Winslow Taylor, Henri Fayol, played an important role during this phase in developing unique principles and theories of management for the finest management practices.

20th Century and Up till Today:

20th Century is the time when management and leadership got its recognition as it was understood by all natures of organizations, companies, industries, government, non government sectors, employers and employees that it is not possible to run any nature of operations smoothly without correct management practices and leadership. Though the importance of management practices and leadership was noticed during Post Industrial Revolution but up till today the world is struggling for correct management and leadership practices that is why we see so much issues in different nature of organizations like; stressed employees, discontent employees which results the biggest issue known as Employee Turnover.

Some Facts

Almost Half of Worldwide Employees Discontented in Jobs; Kelly Services' 2013 Annual Survey

As per staffing agency Kelly Services' annual survey covering 120,000 respondents worldwide, a staggering 48 percent of employees are discontented in their existing jobs, up from 47 percent the previous year (2012).

As per Kelly Services spokesperson "Direct managers and supervisors have a pivotal role in influencing job satisfaction and retention, but many are not heeding the warnings."

"It is sometimes said that employees don't leave companies, they leave managers. What employees are saying is that they want their managers to open up with them and better explain responsibilities and expectations."

"Managers who concentrate on improving communications and providing more opportunities for personal development will have a better chance of maximizing their investment in people and skills."

The employee turnover is the biggest threat of nearly every organization in the world

Research shows millions of employees worldwide are looking for job change. Employee turnover have become biggest threat of nearly every organization in the world as it is costly; statistics shows employee turnover can cost an organization up to 33 percent of an employee's total compensation, together with wages and benefits. The impact, however, is not only financial but a research also shows that employee turnover leaves highly negative impact on other employees.

Main reasons for employee turnover are:

1. Low job satisfaction
2. Lack of appreciation and motivation
3. Lack of understanding with supervisor/manager or co-workers
4. Ineffective or Rude supervisor/ manager or management
5. Inadequate skills and abilities to handle existing profile.
6. Lack of growth opportunities
7. Organizational instability
8. Downturn Organization /Industry
9. Got better opportunity
10. Changed personal or professional circumstances

Source: Kelly Services

WORKPLACE—PRISON COMPARISON

There is a funny comparison of work—prison that employees often tell each other "Prisons are better than workplace" they share their frustration comparing both like this:

In prison you get time off for good behavior.

At work you get rewarded for good behavior with more work.

In prison there are sadistic wardens.

At work, we have managers.

May be that's funny to some people. But now you're willing to know the way to become the proficient manager, it's your responsibility to create healthy and happy workplace which can never be compared with prison.

INTRODUCTION

Everybody Manages. Everybody manage something or other like time, funds, careers, personal and professional relationship etc. We never think of these activities as managing or of ourselves as being manager but the truth is; we all are managers. These examples of managing or being manager are quite easy and simple. So, it is not required to go more in depth to understand that we all our managers and I am sure most of you will agree to this.

Before getting started reading this book it is important to understand what does "Proficient Manager" definition is? What does it mean? Before you go reading further pause and think for a minute . . . What does it mean?

Ok! Let's get started

Who is a Proficient Manager?

Let's separate both words "Proficient" and "Manager" to see what they mean separately and together. According to Oxford Dictionary **"Proficient"** is: competent or skilled in doing or using something, whereas as **"Manager"** is: a person responsible for controlling or administering an organization or group of staff.

So combining the definitions together Proficient Manager is the competent or skilled person responsible for controlling or administering an organization or group of staff.

There are many factors that separate average managers from the proficient managers. In most cases, a person becomes a manager due to working their way up the company ladder; however, being the proficient manager is more than just being knowledgeable of your company's products or services.

But even more importantly, many managers lack the values, skills, feelings, and work etiquettes etc. Functional/technical skills and techniques are easier to learn, but values, beliefs, attitude and behavior are much harder to learn. You will need the management and leadership skills, knowledge along with some other skills and abilities to become the proficient manager.

There has been lot of research about what organizations are looking in their existing and potential managers; typically qualification, functional/technical skills and experience alone is never enough.

In addition to the core competencies, employers want to see skills, abilities and work behavior like:

- Respect
- Optimism
- Communication Skills
- Leadership
- Organized
- Informed and Updated
- Customer Service
- Networking
- Health and Fitness
- Societal Responsibilities

These skills, abilities and behavior are "generic" which means they are required for almost all types of employment. The way in which generic skills are demonstrated depends on the necessity of the particular profession but these are important for both formal managerial positions and informal managerial positions.

The 21st century manager becomes or called proficient manager when he/she is packed with these generic skills, abilities and work behavior.

The critical difference between "Just a Manager" and "Proficient Manager" is:

Just a Manager:

He/she may be enjoying his/her position in hierarchy as he/she has required functional/technical skills along with minimum required experience or qualification but:

- Is the boss who is not always respected, especially behind his/her back
- Is not efficient enough to increase performance and productivity without upsetting their teams. Because they are too bossy.
- They mostly fail to balance their professional and personal life.
- They almost criticize everything and look for reasons to blame someone to get rid of problems
- They are not capable of keeping everyone happy and satisfied
- They care much about themselves and are mainly concerned about their growth
- They increase employee turnover as their teams are never satisfied and happy working with them. They hardly give opportunities and recognition to their team and, that is why their people prefer to switch to new job.

Proficient Manager:

He/she is happy with his/her position in hierarchy as he/she has required functional/technical skills, experience, qualification along with generic skills, abilities and work behavior and:

- Is the leader who is always respected, even behind his/her back
- Is efficient to increase performance and productivity without upsetting their teams.
- They maintain balance in their professional and personal life.
- They never criticize anything; they accept mistakes and learn from them.
- They are capable of keeping everyone happy and satisfied
- They care about everyone and they contribute to their team career growth.
- They increase employee retention as their teams are satisfied and happy working with them. They give opportunities and recognition to their team and, that is why their people prefer not to switch to new job and, even are ready to sacrifice financial benefits that they might get switching the job.

The fact that you are reading this shows you not only have the interest and desire to succeed in management, but truly wish to be a proficient manager.

TOP 10 MISTAKES EVEN GOOD MANAGERS MAKE

Despite having enormous experience few managers lack essential skills in leading and managing teams. The top 10 management and leadership mistakes managers can avoid doing that can help them become successful proficient manager, and highly respected by their team.

1. Lack of Communication:

Lack of communication often leads to conflicts, issues and misunderstandings. Poor communication can create issues like poor team work, lack of understanding of roles and responsibilities, rumors and gossips etc. A manager must recognize how important it is to keep their team in the loop by providing them as much information as possible about missions or changes in the work environment.

Don'ts:

- Don't hide important information, resources, and updates.
- Don't hesitate to give and take feedbacks.

2. Too Friendly or Too Bossy:

Be balanced, don't become too friendly even though you feel you can get along better nor be too bossy even when you feel you are completely of different wave length. It is very essential for manager to maintain balance as it is good to be friendly and bossy but in limits as doing so will keep you and your team respectful and comfortable.

Too Friendly Don'ts:

- Don't get too involved in their personal problems or lives.
- Don't ever crack vulgar and offensive jokes in any circumstances.

Too Bossy Don'ts:

- Don't keep insulting and suggesting your team because you are their boss.
- Don't assign your personal or family work to your team.

3. Believing You Have All The Answers:

If you believe you have all the answers then you are absolutely wrong. Managers with great experience generally make mistake of not listening and taking opinions from others, especially when it comes from juniors. By listening others we make others feel important and respected, even good managers don't have all the answers and they are not ashamed to admit it.

Don'ts:

- Don't fool yourself by believing that you know everything, learn everyday as learning is continuous process.
- Don't miss the opportunity of taking suggestions from others as their suggestion may act beneficial.

4. Making False Promises:

Managers should be very careful before making any promises to their team members. Many managers make promises like a promotion, salary hike, incentives or bonus, holidays etc to get their targets and work done. Don't make promises if you can't fulfill it, false promises can result loss of credibility and respect forever, which may even result into Human Resource complaint.

Don'ts:

- Don't ever make promises which are against company policies and protocol.

5. Being Selfish and Taking All The Credit:

Sometimes managers become selfish and take all the credit for things they have not done, they publicize their name on ideas, targets, achievements and presentations etc that their team worked on. The manager has to realize that their team credit is their credit, a principled proficient manager does not take credit from their team; they in fact honor their team and motivate team to perform better.

Don'ts:

- Don't forget manager is a leader of their team therefore team achievement is their achievement.

6. Showing Favoritism and Not Treating Everyone Equally:

Showing favoritism to anybody for any cause is incorrect. Managers should always treat their employees equally and no decision good or bad should ever be based on factors like; age, gender, caste, religion, favorite or not favorite etc. Showing favoritism and not treating everyone equally can harm work culture which will just lead to lack of motivation, misunderstanding, hatred, troubles and conflicts etc. So it is essential for good managers to promote and follow path of justice.

Don'ts:

- Don't play favorites in employees in any circumstances.
- Don't take decisions that are based on favoritism or inequality.

7. Not Trusting Your Employees:

Many managers don't trust their employees so they end up giving work to only few trusted employees or try doing it themselves. Due to lack of trust managers mostly demotivate and create lack of confidence among few whereas, on other hand they stress and overburden few by not distributing work equally. So it is necessary to trust employees because they will only learn, improve and take responsibilities when they will be trusted and given chance.

Don't:

- Don't distrust employees because they are new.
- Don't hesitate to give employees a chance to prove themselves even if they failed to prove it in past.

8. Not Accepting Responsibilities and Not Defining Responsibilities:

Once you become manager it is your job to understand your responsibilities and define responsibilities to your employees. It is extremely essential for both manager and their team to know their goals along with their missions and visions. In order to have effective working it is necessary that managers should communicate with their employees and discuss each other's job description and responsibilities to avoid any future misunderstanding and challenges.

Don'ts:

- Don't hesitate to have a discussion with your team about your and their responsibilities. Discussions will make you understand each other's roles and challenges better.

9. Resisting Change:

In today's fast changing business environment, it's essential to be open to change and learn new things. Be flexible and try new ways of doing things, keep yourself updated about your organization and don't hesitate to take training of products and services with your team.

Don'ts:

- Don't forget change is natural process, don't let your ego stop you from accepting change and learning something new.

10. Respect Team's Personal and Family Life:

Allow your team, time for their family and personal issues. We need to understand we all work to earn for our personal and families needs, so it is important to respect everyone's personal and family life.

Don'ts:

- Don't make your team stay late in office because your personal official work is not yet finished.
- Don't call your employees during non working hours until it is urgent.
- Don't assign official work during holidays until it is urgent.
- Don't stop them from personal and professional opportunities.

1

RESPECT

R espect is the first rule of successful management, if as a manager you are not getting the respect you deserve than something is seriously incorrect with your leadership. Being manager of organization doesn't mean that you have earned respect because you are on top and leading many people.

It is observed that the main reason why managers don't earn respect is because of their own attitude and behavior, and sometimes they get fake respect which is out of fear because of their position and power, in both the cases situation is severe when managers get No Respect or get Fake Respect. The organization where manager is not respected or been respected out of fear has lack of understanding, blame culture, low productivity and hate zone like atmosphere.

If you are happy and satisfied with respect you get out of fear than let me share a short story called "Fear is Not Respect", hope this story will help you understand difference between fear and respect.

Fear is Not Respect

Long time ago there was a brutal king. King used to treat his people with disrespect and citizens of his kingdom were afraid of him. King had a dog named "Kimo", which he loved more than anything in the world. One morning he found "Kimo" dead and he was really upset. To pay his tribute to "Kimo" he organized last rites for his dog. People from all around his kingdom came for king's dog cremation and conveyed their sincere condolence to the king.

The King was really happy to see that people have great respect and love for him and that is why they gathered for his dog's cremation. King believed he is the most admired king in the world.

After few days the king falls ill, during his illness everybody use to go to see him and wish him speedy recovery thinking he will recover but one day king died, but no one came for his funeral.

This story of brutal king teaches us that respect has to be earned; people may respect you out of fear but respect and fear are two different emotions.

Respect is something you can't ask for. Earning employees respect isn't always easy, but is the most essential quality that is required by managers to perform efficiently as it is said "Respect is the First Rule of Successful Management".

Respect just not makes everyone feel good and comfortable of each other but respect at workplace increase productivity, keep morale high and in fact acts as energy.

Law of Respect:

Respect works similar to Newton's law of motion: "Every Action has an Equal and Opposite Reaction." Here's how it works: if you give respect to someone, he/she gives you same or even more respect incase he/she still doesn't give you than you may consider he/she lacks in basic moral values.

Have You Ever Heard or Said These Lines?

"I will listen to you if you talk to me respectfully"

"I am ready to do this for you if you respectfully ask me"

"He/she is always so humble and respectful to me that is why I want to help him/her"

I am sure every one of us must have heard or said these lines; these lines are clear evidence that we are ready to listen, consider, work and do anything if we are treated respectfully.

Ask Yourself:

Q1. Is earning and giving respect difficult?

Q2. Do we look small or inferior when we talk respectfully to people down in a hierarchy?

Q3. Do you believe that to take work it is important to leave respect aside and use abusive language or show disrespect in any form?

Take few minutes and sincerely ask yourself these questions.

If You Have Answered These Questions Than Let Me Tell

You:

- "Respect Children", "Respect Elders", "Respect Teachers, Respect Your Classmates, Respect Bus Driver and Respect Everyone". I am sure we all have learned this in school then why we forget this golden rule of respect and find it difficult to respect everyone? No school in this world has ever taught about any category of human that should not be treated respectfully, so respect everyone.
- You look big, superior and sophisticated when you talk respectfully and respect everyone.
- Respect works on simple formula: "Give Respect to Earn Respect". So if you want to earn it start giving it first.
- Respect is the driving energy, this will help you increase productivity and achieve targets.
- Respect is the foundation of healthy communication and we all know everything in this world starts with communication.
- Using abusive language or showing disrespect in any form is wrong and it will never help you increase productivity.
- By using disrespectful ways of taking work, you make your team members just pretend as they are affected but they will not work hard to achieve goals because you are damaging their self esteem.

So to be respectful proficient manager it is necessary for managers to create respectful atmosphere at workplace, which can only be possible if they practice respectful behavior towards others and convey their people how respectful behavior towards each other can make their working comfortable, satisfying and dynamic.

TIPS FOR MANAGERS—THAT WILL HELP YOU EARN RESPECT

Respect Yourself:

Always treat yourself with respect, have strong values that you can be proud of and stand for them no matter what happens. When you treat yourself with respect, you project an image of respectability.

Trust Your People:

Managers can't do everything themselves. Managers should trust their people and must demonstrate trust. Empower your people to make their own decisions and judgments.

Treat Everyone Equally:

Don't be racist; sexist or fanatic. You must treat everyone equally and respectfully.

Communicate:

Communicate regularly with your team members, management and customers. Keep them informed on latest updates and talk sometime for no reasons to ask how they are doing.

Speak Respectfully:

Never use abusive language this is a terrible mistake most managers make and lose their respect for ever.

Don't Use Disrespectful Body Language:

Make sure you never use any disrespectful body language like showing slap or finger, pinching, bunching, pressing hand tightly or touching etc.

Honor Your Promises:

Always keep your words, be honest and deliver what you promised. This will increase your esteem in eyes of others and people will trust you, after all trust is respect.

Be Objective:

If someone is rude to you and it's bothering you, please think carefully before reacting and ask yourself: what's really bothering you? Rudeness or Honesty

Influence with Humbleness:

If someone is rude don't behave in same way as it will only worsen the situation. Control your emotions and don't let them control you, keep calm and be respectful because your behavior may influence the rude person.

Don't Be Hypocrite:

If you have made rules at work place make sure you follow them or else you will look hypocrite.

THE PARROTS STORY

There is a story of customer who goes to pet shop to buy a parrot. The customer asked the sales assistant that I am looking to buy parrot, can you please help me buy a parrot? The assistant takes the customer to the parrot section of the pet shop and asked him to choose any parrot of his choice.

Customer: How old is yellow parrot and how much it cost?

Sales Assistant: Yellow parrot is 3 years old and it is for $ 2000.

Customer: Why is it so expensive? (Shocked and Surprised)

Sales Assistant: Sir, this parrot is very special as he knows typing and he types really fast.

Customer: What about Green one?

Sales Assistant: Green parrot is 4 years old is for $ 5000 and he knows typing, can talk, take notes and can answer the incoming phone calls.

Customer: Good, what about Red one?

Sales Assistant: Red one is 3 years old and is for $ 10,000.

Customer: Why? What does he do?

Sales Assistant: I don't know, but other two really respect him and call him "gentlemen".

This short funny story about respect and leadership teaches us that it is the respect from everyone that makes us look better, superior and valuable. Therefore to increase your value and worth, give respect to earn respect.

Think Page

Think and write down your plans and thoughts that you have made after reading this chapter. This "Think Page" will help you create an action plan and ideas that you can use to bring change and improvement in your life to be proficient manager.

Space above is intentionally left blank. Use blank space to write your ideas and plans

2

OPTIMISM

"A man is but the product of his thoughts. What he thinks, he becomes"—Mahatma Gandhi

According to Merriam-Webster Dictionary "Optimism" is a doctrine that, this world is the best possible world And "Pessimism" is the doctrine that reality is essentially evil.

Pessimism in the workplace is the serious concern these days. Almost everybody is surrounded by worries, workload, personal—professional commitments and activities etc, all these pressures make us think and behave pessimistically.

Workplace optimism or pessimism is contagious. When one employee experiences something good or bad he/she shares the same with their coworkers and this creates positivity or negativity at workplace.

Optimism is the quality that every employee of any organization has to have. Optimism is the foundation of success and motivation, it is an energy that opens many opportunities, helps you deal with challenges, work efficiently and creates healthier relationships.

Many studies have shown that manager's optimism actually contribute to productivity, efficiency of their team and organization as whole. According to Seligman (2002, p.83) "optimism and hope cause better resistance to depression when bad events strike, better performance at work, particularly in challenging jobs and better physical health."

So in today's business environment managers have very vital role to play, it is the responsibility of managers to cure negativity and control the situations that causes pessimism. Optimism at workplace is not just feel good factor but it is the factor that results healthy—positive workplace with better productivity and employee's satisfaction.

Workplace optimism is a culture created by managers, so managers must keep themselves and their team positive. There are few initiatives managers can apply that will increase morale, productivity, and decrease stress, ensuing positivity at workplace.

- ➤ Treat everyone respectfully and equally.
- ➤ Share information that can affect productivity.
- ➤ Know your people and try to take work as per their abilities.
- ➤ Create positive attitude of problem solving with no blaming rule.
- ➤ Talk to people who are pessimist and try to resolve their concerns.

Tips to Stay Optimistic

Trust Yourself:

Never underestimate yourself, something if others can do so can you. Talk to people who appreciate you and your skills as their presence will help you trust yourself more.

Stay Busy:

Keeping yourself busy is the best way to positivity as it is said; idle mind is devil's workshop. Make sure to keep yourself busy with positive activities.

Share Your Feelings:

Share your opinions, problems and sorrows with people you trust. This will keep you feel better as your close ones suggestions and motivations will keep you remain positive.

Exercise Everyday:

Exercise helps you remain optimistic as it is the way of keeping yourself in shape. It is observed people who exercise everyday are not just healthy and strong but in most of the cases they are happier as workout fights depression.

Surround Yourself with Positive People:

The people around you influence the way you think. If you are in the company of people with negativity sooner or later their views can influence your thinking too, therefore surround yourself with people with positive attitude as their optimism will support you and will help you understand the opportunities.

Take Short Breaks:

It is good to stay busy to remain optimist but over busyness can make you think and behave pessimist, thus take short breaks of few minutes. Do something you love; talk to your friends or loved ones, watch short interesting clipping or videos, listen to a song, play video game, read jokes etc. These breaks are not going to waste your time in fact this will help you utilize time better as you will work more efficiently, perform positive and feel fresh after these short breaks.

Read and Watch Positive Inspiring Stories:

One of the finest ways to stay optimistic is by reading and watching positive inspiring stories or movies. Inspiring motivating quotes, articles, stories and movies will help you think and behave positive.

STORY OF PESSIMIST AND OPTIMIST

You must have heard or read old famous story of pessimist and optimist that illustrates the difference between pessimist and optimist.

On an autumn evening in London, British Shoe manufacturer management called up a meeting with all their Sales Managers from all regions of Europe. The company was looking to expand business globally, after a full day of meeting with their Sales Managers, management shortlisted two sales managers to travel to Africa to investigate and report back on market potential.

Both Sales Managers travelled to Africa and explored shoe market potential. When they returned back to London after few weeks, this is how they reported:

Management: So what you think is there any potential in Africa?

1st Sales Manager: "There is no potential in Africa as nobody wears shoes"

2nd Sales Manager: "There is a very big potential in Africa as nobody wears shoes, I think we can be first mover and gain extremely high market share."

This is a short simple story that shows how a single situation is viewed in two different ways. We can see how both managers viewed the same situation differently "No Body Wears Shoes in Africa", where 1st Manager was completely pessimist and believes that there is no opportunity in Africa whereas, 2nd Manager was completely optimistic and believes there is opportunity in Africa. This story is a good example to learn how optimism can open opportunities and generates profits.

BRICKLAYER STORY

There is a story about three bricklayers. Each bricklayer was asked, "What are you doing?"

The first replied, "Laying brick."

The second answered, "Making $9.30 an hour."

And the third said, "Me? Why, I'm building the world's greatest cathedral."

We become what we think about and having a bigger perspective on our work makes us bigger.

Let's raise a toast so that we may & we have the capacity to think optimistically, and in turn, live positively.

THINK PAGE

Think and write down your plans and thoughts that you have made after reading this chapter. This "Think Page" will help you create an action plan and ideas that you can use to bring change and improvement in your life to be proficient manager.

Space above is intentionally left blank. Use blank space to write your ideas and plans

3

COMMUNICATION SKILLS

One of the biggest challenges managers face is communication. Nearly every other skill depends on communication therefore communication is also one of the most important characteristic of leadership. Effective verbal and nonverbal communication skills are important at workplace. Many organizations spend a lot of money to train their people on how to effectively communicate since they know being able to communicate efficiently is a most important of all life skills.

Managers without communication skills can fail to gain commitment from their people, fail to achieve goals and fail to develop understanding. In short, they fail overall no matter how good their intention maybe.

Good communication skills are vital for managers to carry out their roles effectively as it is tool for conveying information, ideas, and opinions. The proficient manager should be able to communicate many things to many people; he/she must communicate efficiently at all levels and with all sort of people like their team, individuals, dealers, producers, customers, financers and bosses etc.

Good and effective communication makes manager's role easier as it is the prime way of decision making, improving teamwork, sorting out issues, problem solving and understanding and explaining diversity. Effective verbal communication mainly combines set of skills like listening, speaking and reading, so it is crucial that managers should master these skills to convey their message effectively.

These skills cannot be mastered in few days; it takes time and effort to develop these skills to be proficient communicator. Managers can enhance their communication skills with dedication and practice using a few key strategies that will assist decide what, when and how to communicate successfully.

Mastering Domestic and Global Language

Mastering the language in which these skills takes place is the first and the most important step to develop communication skills. We all are aware that each country has their own language to communicate as France has French, Germany has German, China has Chinese, USA has English and most of other countries have their own language or English language as their official language. Managers must master their national and official languages along with the English language because the fact is that English language has become global corporate and business language.

With the continuous increasing global business dealings the need for effective communication to meet global business demand has also increased and therefore brands have adopted global language for their businesses. Global market leaders like Samsung, Toyota, Renault, Audi and Mercedes etc even have adopted English as their main language of business accepting the fact that to be global they need global language too to expand beyond borders.

Mastering Body Language

Along with language the skill that managers should learn to communicate effectively is the body language. Body language refers to the nonverbal signs that we use to communicate and these signs are included in our communication even during verbal communication. Understanding body language is important as wrong gestures can convey wrong message during both listening and speaking. Managers should know and understand that gesture like eye contact, facial gesture, hand movement and these similar actions play critical role in communication. Body language can make or destroy the communication, so developing your awareness of the signs of body language is important as it will help you and others to communicate more effectively with you.

Communication for Growth

As every one of us want to grow more and more, thus to execute growth we must never stop learning and should develop the fundamental skills along with the skills for communication.

The three language skills: listening, speaking and writing are all correlated skills. Many people think that communication is all about speaking, however while speaking you require listener as it is a two-way process and none of these skills can be mastered alone, thus the entire set of these skills should be considered important as it only make sense when the recipient of your message understands you.

Tips to Improve Your Body Language

Hygiene and Grooming:

You might think that clothes, hygiene and grooming are unimportant, but you are wrong. Personal hygiene and grooming are the vital step of effective body language as your general appearance makes huge impact on people. Thus, it is very important that you:

- Wear neat and ironed clothes
- Your mouth and body should not smell bad, in fact wear fragrance
- Shoes should be polished
- Men should shave everyday and if you don't shave keep your beard trimmed
- Both men and women should wear professional hairstyle

Perfect Handshake:

Your handshake should not be too pumping, shaking, tied or loose. A handshake should be firm and must not last more than 5 seconds both in case of males and females.

Smile but Don't Laugh:

Always have smile on your face as it keeps you and people around you happy. A smile will always make you look friendly, neutral and open minded.

Make Eye Contact but Don't Stare:

Eyes speaks, eye contact during communication makes communication effective. Keep balanced eye contact, too much might be seen as intense and may be seen as staring.

Don't Stand or Sit Too Close:

No touching other than handshake should happen at workplace. Always maintain personal space and never sit or stand too close to anyone.

Keep Hands Out of Your Pocket:

Keep your hands out of your pocket, this is considered rude and make you look uncomfortable or unsure of yourself.

Stand and Sit Straight:

Standing and sitting straight is not only good for your back and body but good for communication too. This shows you are active and interested in communicating which definitely create positivity.

Don't Cross Legs and Arms:

You possibly have already heard this: you shouldn't cross your arms and legs as it might make you look protective. But the proper professional stance is to keep your arms right at your sides.

PROFICIENT LISTENER

The proficient manager is a proficient listener. Managers who listen carefully and effectively are proficient communicators as they know and understand their customers, team and people in hierarchy better. Active listening combined with trying to understand other's viewpoint is the most successful form of listening.

By listening to someone carefully will not only help you understand someone's ideas and opinions better but also show respect which helps to build and maintain relationships. To be excellent listener at workplace you must be aware of industry jargons and should have excellent analytical skills.

Proficient Manager treats everyone equally and listens open-mindedly because listening is all about variety of ideas, opinions and creativity, thus listen to know, understand and learn.

TIPS TO BECOME PROFICIENT LISTENER

Be Silent:

It is not just a tip but also a part of good habit to be silent when someone is speaking and by being silent you will be able to listen and understand speaker better. "Listen More and Speak Less" should be key phrase for every manager.

Remove Distractions:

Don't get distracted by objects, gadgets, mobile phones, by your own thoughts or by talking to someone on your side as it will break your concentration to listen and this can even distract speaker.

Eye Contact:

Eye contact is form of body language which is important for communication as we don't listen just from ears, so it is necessary to have eye contact with speaker for successful listening and understanding. But make sure you maintain the eye contact to the degree that both listener and speaker remain comfortable.

Recognize Body Language:

Recognize both verbal and non verbal language, such as tone, facial expressions, hand movement and other body language. Try to understand what else is said by body language as sometimes lot is said by body language alone.

Be Open Minded:

You can only listen to someone carefully when you are open minded, that means you are ready to listen to a speaker without judging him/her on basis of gender, experience, love, hatred or because of any professional/personal reasons.

Ask Questions:

It is good to ask questions for clarification but make sure you only ask questions when speaker pauses as otherwise it would be consider as interrupting.

Don't Interrupt:

Most of the times people interrupt the speaker, this practice is dangerous for both speaker and listener. Interrupting sometimes can cause big misunderstanding so be patient and wait for speaker to complete.

PROFICIENT SPEAKER

The proficient manager is a proficient speaker. Similar to listening, speaking is another necessary skill for effective communication. A good speaker has many qualities some of which are learned and some are born. The most essential skill to be good speaker is to be good listener because who listens well can speak well.

Speaking is the skill of communication that will help managers to convey their mind and heart. It's not necessary to know big and difficult words to be good speaker. In fact people who use much of difficult and big words especially jargons fails to convey their message effectively. The point of speaking is to convey and share information, and to have two-way exchange. The managers are called proficient speaker when they are capable of conveying and sharing important information efficiently like; targets, responsibilities, visions, missions, ideas, opinions, specifications and features etc and they should be able to speak confidently and efficiently with everyone.

But good speaking skills are not just about speaking. Proficient speaker encourages others to share opinions and information that enable the two-way exchange. Speaking skills are important for managers whether it be communicating one on one or to a team. So, this skill must be mastered by managers to be proficient manager.

Tips to Become Proficient Speaker

Study Your Listeners:

It is essential for managers to study their listeners they are addressing. Different type of listeners may require different techniques of speech, and for successful speech you must develop a connection with the listeners which is possible if you studied your listeners.

Control Your Voice:

Speaker must know when and when not to speak loudly as different places may need different volumes. To be good speaker it is essential to know how to present your voice, when to pause and at what pitch to speak. One can know these details by taking feedback from close ones and by watching or by listening to their speech recordings.

Eye Contact:

Eye contact is form of body language which is important for communication as we also speaks through our eyes. Eye contact is one way to increase your engagement with an audience and get feedback from your audience.

Enthusiasm and Body Language:

Managers should speak with enthusiasm to keep listeners energized. They must have correct and positive body language because it is believed that over 70% of communication happens through body language and only 30% is verbal, thus body language should be encouraging.

Amaze Your Listeners:

Find amazing stats, facts or analogy correlated to your topic that can surprise and excite everyone. Meaningful information, facts and analogy can grab everyone's attention and bring clarity.

Tell A Story:

A listener listens better if the speaker tells everything in story form rather than in boring way. Although not everything can be described in story format but if possible speaker should try to tell stories that can help listeners to understand better, excites them, motivates them and touches them in the way to want it to happen.

Pause:

Pauses are the most important part of speech as Sir Ralph Richardson once said, *"The most precious things in speech are the pauses."* Proficient speakers use the pause effectively. A pause can grab attention, gives time to both listener and speaker to think and relax. It is also noticed that people who pause appropriately never use expressions like "Um", "Naa" "haa" etc.

Accept Truth:

It is hard to accept truth but it is always good to accept mistakes and admit that you don't know everything. When you accept truth and the fact you don't know everything, it makes the audience pay greater respect and attention to you.

TELEPHONE COMMUNICATION

Businesses prefer telephone for communication as they are instant way of communicating. Telephone calls are part of everyday work; it is hard to imagine a business without a telephone in fact for most of the businesses telephone is the primary point of contact.

The telephone also offers a more personal approach than email, text messaging or letters. You can respond to question and answers on the spot when using telephone for communication. Technologies like face-to-face calling via HangOuts, MSN, Yahoo, and Skype etc have made calling even more popular as many of these providers offer free or affordable price calling.

Many businesses are completely based on telephones like call centre, BPOs etc and few businesses are dependent on telephone for their customer service and support.

Effective telephone communication involves listening and speaking skills with telephone etiquettes. Even the most correct and valuable information loses its value and meaning if not delivered efficiently with correct skills and etiquettes. Thus, we may say that every manager should know how to apply the correct telephonic techniques to get most out of this communication tool in business.

Tips for Effective Telephone Communication

Greet & Identify Yourself:

Always start the conversation by greeting "Hello" "Good Morning" "Good Afternoon" followed by your company name or your name further or followed by department if required.

Speak Nicely & Slowly:

Make sure you speak nicely that means you must sound pleasant and along with speaking nicely one must speak slowly for clarity.

Stay Calm:

Even if you are in hurry talk calmly and if urgent request call back or commit call back but don't rush the talk.

Never Interrupt:

Never interrupt while someone is talking as it creates confusion and makes conversation rough. Pause after completing your sentence, this gives time to other person to respond and grab information.

Don't Distract:

Never distract yourself and person on another side by chewing, eating, turning papers, using gadgets or by speaking with someone else. Distractions make communication ineffective and unpleasant.

Avoid Loud Speaker:

Although loud speakers are designed to talk but until it is not required urgently avoid using speaker feature as it makes conversation uncomfortable and unpleasant.

End a Call Respectfully:

Be sure you complete the conversation before ending the call, and always end the call respectfully—"It was nice talking you—Bye" "Have a Good Day—Bye".

Examples of Good Telephone Conversation:

Hello/Good Morning, I am Richard Parker, calling on behalf of RBS. > Followed by conversation > It was nice talking to you. Have a good day—Bye (End Call Respectfully)

Proficient Writer

The proficient manager is proficient writer. Similar to listening and speaking, writing is a vital skill for effective communication as managerial communication still ends up on paper. Now a day's managers have to write so much like writing various types of reports, articles, advertisements, emails and text message etc.

It is very easy for some managers to speak, but when it comes to writing they fail to present their ideas and respond effectively to the needs of others. Writing cannot be avoided; excellent writing is the result of excellent planning and clear thoughts, thus manager must know their purpose of writing and should know their readers as communication in any form is two-way exercise.

The popular practices of writing for managers are presentations, emails and text messaging. Managers have to be excellent in creating presentations, writing emails and writing text messages to convey their messages efficiently and professionally.

EFFECTIVE E MAILS

In today's business world email is the most important form of written communication; emails are preferred as they are easy, quick and formal. Emails are the lifeline of businesses these days as managers get and give every kind of information, updates, approvals, rejections and other remarks or opinions using this mode of communication, thus it is necessary for managers to write effectively to convey their messages correctly and accurately.

Managers should be very careful while writing and must exercise email etiquettes because of the following reasons:

Effectiveness:

Emails should be written to the point and must have all the essential details to convey the message effectively.

Professionalism:

It is important you write emails professionally using correct language and spelling as emails just don't convey message but also convey yours and your company's professional image.

Commitment:

Your emails can act as your written commitment, so you should be very alert while writing. Avoid writing anything incorrect or impossible as these commitments may result into misunderstanding and disputes.

Monitoring Policy:

Companies these days monitor their employee's emails so managers must follow email etiquettes and respect company's email policies.

Email Etiquette Tips

Don't Ignore Subject:

You must fill in the subject line with accurate subject as the first thing receiver reads is the subject, and it's the subject that makes email look important or unimportant.

Don't Ignore Salutation:

Your email must open by addressing with correct salutation. Salutation should not be ignored even if you are writing to your colleagues who are your friends. Thus, your email should always begin with salutation.

Examples:

- o Respected Sir or Respected Madam or Respected Sir/ Madam
- o Dear Sir/Madam,
- o Dear Prof. Peter, or Dear Dr. Smith,
- o Hello Jamie,

Always use formal salutation while writing professional emails and you must have some space between salutation and paragraph.

Short and Precise Paragraphs:

Emails are effective if they are short and precise. While writing emails try to come directly to point keeping paragraphs short and use bullets or numbering for better clarity.

Read and Use Spell Check:

You must read email and use spell check before sending email as your incorrect sentencing and wrong spelling may change the sense of your email resulting embarrassment, misunderstanding or dispute.

Don't Ignore Signature:

Your email have to end with some polite words like "Thanks & Regards" "Yours Sincerely" etc. and must have all essential details like your Name, Designation, Department (in case if it's their) and Contact details.

Thanks & Regards

Richard Fryer
Relationship Manager
Business Banking Department
T: +44—736-XXXX (Extension: 7563)

Avoid writing saying and quotes in the footer of your email if they don't belong to you or your company as they look extra.

Email Format Sample:

Respected Sir,

Allow me to introduce myself, I am Amanda Purple and I am Customer Relationship Manager,

_____
_____
_____
_____
_____

We have following plans:

1. Option A
2. Option B

Please don't hesitate to contact me for any further information.

Thanks & Regards

Amanda Purple
Chief Finance Officer,
Proficient Manager Institute,
North Street, Bedminster,
Bristol, United Kingdom
Telephone: +44 7250-XXXX, Fax: +44 7260-XXXX

EFFECTIVE TEXT MESSAGES

Text messaging has become one of the popular way of communicating because of the innovation in smart phone technology. Applications likes whatsApp, Line, We Chat, Hangouts, BBM and similar kind of applications and messengers have made text messaging more convenient and accepted as you can send and receive files, picture and can do lot more with them.

Although text messaging has become popular you should try to avoid if possible and should prefer to use email or making call rather than sending text messaging. Text messaging are limited to certain number of words and it becomes difficult to communicate with such limitations especially when you are sending text without using any of latest messenger application like WhatsApp, We chat etc.

But if you are using text messaging for your professional use for any reason that you can't or don't want to avoid using it then in that case you must follow some tips to make your text messages effective and formal.

Tips for Effective Text Messaging

Use Salutation:

You must use salutation while sending professional messages as they keep the text polite and formal.

Avoid Shortcuts:

You should avoid using shortcuts and abbreviations like "u" (for "You") "Thnx" (for "Thanks") "LOL" (for "Laugh Out Loud") etc.

Shortcuts and abbreviations look cheap, casual and make conversation informal.

Use Punctuation:

Always type your texts using punctuation as you use in writing emails and letters. Messages without punctuation can change the sense of your text.

Use Capital Letters Carefully:

Capital letters should be carefully used while sending text messages. Many people don't like it when their name is written in all lower case, writing names in lower case is consider as taking someone for granted or casually. Always write first alphabet of Name in capital and you must not write complete sentence in capital as it sound SHOUTING and RUDE.

Avoid Sending Urgent and Negative Text:

Never send important and urgent messages by text as it can change the sense making it completely casual and makes it difficult to understand that in which sense you have text.

Example of Urgent and Negative Text:

- Finally you are promoted (Difficult to understand sender's emotion—Is he/she showing happiness or criticizing)

Examples of Informal and Formal Text Messages:

- i hv send u all details by email plz check (Informal)
- Dear Sir, I have send you all details, please check your email. (Formal)

- Can we meet at 5pm 2day to discuss the designs (Informal)
- Hi Jane! Can we meet at 5pm today to discuss the designs? (Formal)

If you carefully observe text messages above you will notice that it doesn't take much to write nice formal and professional text. Greeting, using correct spellings, punctuation will let you keep your professional image.

Think Page

Think and write down your plans and thoughts that you have made after reading this chapter. This "Think Page" will help you create an action plan and ideas that you can use to bring change and improvement in your life to be proficient manager.

Space above is intentionally left blank. Use blank space to write your ideas and plans

4

LEADERSHIP

A manager has various complex responsibilities and has to ensure that all the operations of organization run smoothly and efficiently. Leading is the most imperative skill of management that managers has to have, the manager who is good leader is capable of directing his people much more proficiently and knows how to get work done and by whom.

It is said that, "Leaders Leads and Managers Manages" this has been the subject of almost constant debate for past many years. However, managers and leaders need combination of both management and leadership as both are similar in many respects. There was a time when both managers and leaders roles could be easily separated but in this economic globalization, there is much more complexity at workplace and as a result skills needed for managers and leaders cannot be separated.

Employees in starting of their new jobs or already working employees see their new manager as a leader; it is in the hands of the manager to act like manager or leader. Your team always needs the leader who can guide them, motivate them and put them on right path but unfortunately most of the managers fail to be a leader.

Managerial leadership is usually thought of as the capability of manager to motivate people to achieve organizational targets, but it is not true as managerial leader is never limited to just financial targets. They do much more for the organization and their people and that's what makes them a leader.

Managerial leader benefits organization and their people by creating values, which helps both team and organization to be leader as well.

To understand management and leadership it is important to understand their characteristics. Warren G Bennis an organizational consultant and author widely regarded as pioneer of the contemporary field of leadership. According to Bennis leaders and managers qualities can be categorized as follow:

MANAGERS	LEADERS
• Administers	• Innovators
• Imitates	• Originates
• Maintains	• Develops
• Focuses on Systems and Structures	• Focuses on People
• Relies on Control	• Inspires Trust
• Short-Range View	• Long-Range Perspective
• Asks How and When	• Asks What and Why
• Eyes on the Bottom Line	• Eyes on the Horizon
• Accept the Status Quo	• Change the Status Quo
• Does Things Right	• Does Right Things

* Adapted from Kotter, What Leaders Really Do (1999).

According to John P. Kotter, (2001, Pg.3) "Leadership and management are two distinctive and complementary systems of action. Both are necessary for success in an increasingly complex and volatile business environment."

So, when manager manage as a leader they move towards opportunities. The proficient manager's primary motivation is to work with difference and they know when to step beyond role and lead; they recognize how to differentiate management from leadership.

Ultimately, leadership is an art and ability that manager require to become proficient manager and act as a good leader.

To overcome the challenge of being a leader you can use tips given on next page to enhance your leadership abilities and bring the best out of your people.

Tips for Managers to Become Leaders

Share the Vision:

Share the vision with your people to let them know what you want them to achieve, this will keep your people optimistic and give them a sense of achievement.

Build Relationships:

Manager without leadership skills are never capable of building relationships, that is why it is said: "People Leaves Managers, Not Companies". Relationships are the secret of winning team as it creates understanding, motivation and commitment.

Take Responsibility:

As a manager responsibilities are yours but bad managers know how to put them on others . . . You must learn to take responsibilities for both good and bad things because leaders never blame, they accept mistakes.

Do What You Believe:

Managers become leaders when they do things differently. To act like leader and think like manager do what you believe. Doing what you believe and taking appropriate risks without fear of failure makes manager a good leader.

Be Open-Minded:

Be open-minded and challenge your assumptions. This means you are open to feedbacks even if they look like criticism, a good leader takes feedback positively and learn to examine every situation from many angles. Open-mindedness will help you learn new things and will also open opportunities for you.

Set a Good Example:

You as a leader need to understand that you are watched by your people and they look up to you as a role model. Set a good example and do things that you expect from them with professionalism and honesty. For example, if you expect them to be punctual make sure you are punctual as well.

Stand for Your Values:

Leadership is value based. Have courage to stand up for your values that you believe. Values may make your path difficult but it puts you on right path.

For Example: You are food quality control manager and food production manager is your good friend. You reject food to get packed if food is substandard. This is because you value your values more than anything.

Motivate:

Leadership is not about managing, it is about influencing. As a leader, motivating your employees is path to your success. Leaders knows everyone have different motivational profiles, by tapping into the individual needs of their staff they can maximize efficiency of their people.

MANAGERS WITHOUT & WITH LEADERSHIP TRAITS

I have been observing managers of different organizations and sectors from past many years, and my observations have always disturbed me. Below you will find the difference between managers without and with leadership traits and their behavior towards themselves and others.

Without Leadership Traits:

- ❖ They are mostly autocratic.
- ❖ They impose responsibility.
- ❖ If targets are not achieved they make their teams stay late even after working hours to create work pressure and annoy them to the fullest.
- ❖ They just respect professional life and expect others to behave in the same way.
- ❖ They forget that we earn for ourselves and our family to have better life.

Real Life Example: I remember when I was working with insurance company our channel partner's cluster head use to make his team stay after working hours. The standard working hours were from 9.00 am to 6.30 pm but he made it 8.45 am to 9.00 pm, surprisingly I have never seen anyone doing anything productive in those extra hours.

I still remember his words: *"If you want to grow professionally like me you must give up everything, I have given up my personal life. My wife and children complains every day but I don't care I still work late hours. If I can, why can't you do the same?"*

Result: I have seen more than 40% of his staff changing their jobs in less than 8 months, such manager causes employee turnover.

Consequences: Such manager creates managers like themselves and people who don't like their style of working leave or change the job.

With Leadership Traits:

- ❖ They are democratic.
- ❖ They create a sense of responsibility.
- ❖ If targets are not achieved they still allow their teams to leave after working hours and explain them how important it is to achieve targets to get rid of stress and enjoy our personal space.
- ❖ They respect both professional and personal life and expect others to behave in same way.
- ❖ They know, after all we earn for ourselves and our family to have better life.

Solution to Without Leadership Traits Example: I wish our channel partner's cluster head would have both leadership and management skills. He could have set a good example and should have been capable of demonstrating how one can complete his work within working hours. I wish he could have said this: "If you want to grow and enjoy your life like me, you must learn to work efficiently. I give time to both personal and professional life. My wife and children never complains because I give them time they deserve."

Result: We would have not seen employees changing or leaving their jobs and this would have increased employee retention.

Outcome: Such leader creates leaders like themselves and they are always liked by people.

THINK PAGE

Think and write down your plans and thoughts that you have made after reading this chapter. This "Think Page" will help you create an action plan and ideas that you can use to bring change and improvement in your life to be proficient manager.

Space above is intentionally left blank. Use blank space to write your ideas and plans

5

LEARN TO ORGANIZE EVERYTHING

M anagers often have the heaviest workload. They do much more than managing team and dealing with customers. Managers do lot of things throughout the day in order to make sure that everything runs smoothly and perfectly. To overcome their difficulties without being stressed and anxious it is essential for managers to learn to organize time and everything.

To learn the skill of organizing, understanding its meaning is vital. According to Oxford Dictionary "Organize" means "arrange systematically; order". The ability of arranging everything systematically is the secret of managers to perform at their highest potential. Right practices of managing time and things will save time and energy which can be used to do other productive things.

Managers who are unorganized stress themselves because of their habits and waste most of their time finding small things like stapler, eraser, keys, forms, documents etc. or remembering passwords, important dates and even customer profiles etc.

Keeping things organized is not the skill but the habit, one must know their abilities . . . if you are aware that you forget things easily you must develop a habit of keeping them at one particular place so, you may know where to look for it. Remember management is all about managing so whether it is managing self, team, customers or things you should be able to manage everything that what makes a manager the proficient manager.

Almost every one of us has experienced or else have witness how forgetting things and password becomes so painful that it results loss of money, destruction or waste of time. Thus, writing and keeping password safely, having reminders of appointments and keeping things on their place can help to become organized. So build a habit and start the organizing process . . .

Jack Daniel's Story—Consequences of Being Unorganized

We all know about Jasper Newton Daniel known as Jack Daniel, He was born on a Moore County farm in September 1850. Jasper lost his mother at age of seven and that was the time when his family was undergoing hardships. Jasper was only 10 when his father decided it was time for Jasper to learn trade and he started working. The young Jasper attained his education and learned trade skills working at a store, he learned various skills including brewing of whisky from store owner and he became good and known for it, this was the time when Jasper became popular by his nickname "Jack".

Jack, was only 13 years old when he lost his father but rather then mourning the death of his father he concentrate his time on the business and worked really hard. He at his early teen hired couple of people to help him and at the age of 16 he registered his business with United States government. In 20's Jack was famous with his product known as Jack Daniel's, he thereafter grown and achieved at every step of life.

Jack learned so much in his life from his personal and professional experiences but his small habit of not being organized and repeating his mistake changed his life and history of world's biggest brand. Sometime around 1906, Jack Daniel arrived early to his office and tried to open the safe in his office which contained valuable documents and things. He couldn't recall the combination nor has written down it anywhere knowing the fact that this was not the first time when Jack has forgotten the combination. Jack got really angry and upset with trying wrong combinations again and again, and in his frustration he kicked the safe really hard and broke his toe. Infection soon set up in his toe and he started falling ill.

Jack was badly ill within few months. Jack began turning more and more of the company's operations over to his nephew Lem

Motlow and deeded his business to him. On 9th October 1911, after five years of safe kicking episode Jack died of infection caused by broken toe.

Jack would not have died if he was organized and had written combination somewhere. Habit of being organized would have saved his life.

This story of Jack Daniel teaches us about the consequences of being unorganized. It is important for each of us to be organized both at work and home as we never know what a small issue can change our life forever and ever.

TIPS FOR BEING ORGANIZED

Know What's Happening:

The first thing manager or employee should do after marking their attendance should be checking emails. It is seen that priority emails mostly flash early morning as companies want their people to start their day with priorities. So, if you are not starting your day checking emails and surfing employee information portal than probably you are not planning your day correctly.

Use Technology:

Technology gadgets are full of features. Many of features like reminder, calendar, organizer, planner, alarm, scheduler, address book, auto replier etc. are very useful for planning and organizing. Start using technology smartly and make life easier.

Keep Things in Their Place:

Build a habit of keeping things in their place, use stationary-pen stand for keeping all items at one place, and allocate drawers for all items like forms, documents, sheets etc. In case you easily forget passwords then write down hints of your password and keep it in a safe place away from your computer probably in your wallet, car or somewhere else.

Do Difficult Things First:

Every one of us loves to start our day with easy things and we often waste our energy on doing easy things first. But the secret of completing everything stress free on time is to start your day doing difficult things first as your energy will drop every passing hour and difficult will become even more difficult later.

Keep Essential Things within Reach:

By passing time we come to know what all things are essential for smooth working. Create checklist of essential things that are required every day. For example: If you work at bank make sure you have all types of forms (Account Opening/ Closing/ Fixed Deposit etc.) available with you along with essential stationary like pen, stapler, glue etc. Keeping essential things within reach saves time, increase efficiency and productivity and makes you look professional.

Discard Junk:

If you have collection of useless piles of junk like outdated forms, reports etc on your desk then discard it today. Useless piles not only waste space but also creates confusion, waste time and decrease productivity. If you want to keep something as a record you can keep the scan copy of it if the original copy is not that important or you can keep hard copy somewhere else.

Arrange Everything Before You Leave:

Make sure you arrange everything in order when you're done working for the day. It is good to start day fresh next morning without spending time cleaning your previous day mess. This will save your time and energy.

THINK PAGE

Think and write down your plans and thoughts that you have made after reading this chapter. This "Think Page" will help you create an action plan and ideas that you can use to bring change and improvement in your life to be proficient manager.

Space above is intentionally left blank. Use blank space to write your ideas and plans

6

KEEP YOURSELF AND YOUR TEAM INFORMED

In most organizations managers are the vital link between management and team, they work closely with everyone that is why they play important role in providing information that is essential for customers, team and management. In that sense it is the responsibility of managers ensuring that business runs smoothly. In order to have smooth operations, increased productivity, and for success information sharing is very crucial.

If you are manager and you are unable to take out information or not sharing information then you are not doing your job efficiently. The biggest lesson Insurance company job taught me was the importance of sharing information. I remember after few months of my job suddenly insurance company changed their policy regarding use of black ink for filling application forms. I and my co-workers were never informed by territory manager regarding the change that stated "Use Only Blue Ink", unfortunately the same week our channel partners sold insurances worth million of rupees. Unluckily all application forms were filled out in black ink.

All applications were denied by the company. I discussed the matter with territory manager and she said "Oh I forgot to forward email regarding these changes". After realizing her mistake she forwarded me email, shockingly original email was almost 10 days old.

I looked unprofessional in front of our channel partners as we could not manage to get few applications filled again. Because of this loss I was criticized for weeks by channel partners. I had no choice; I apologized for mistake I never was responsible for.

As per Henry Mintzberg internationally renowned academic and author on business and management has described ten managerial roles out of which informational role is one of the important managerial role. According to Henry managers must generate and share information effectively to attain organizational targets. He has listed three roles under informational roles, which consist of monitor, disseminator and spokesperson.

Monitor:

In monitoring role managers gathers the information that can affect productivity of employees and organization; they collect information by upward, downward and horizontal communication. They also gather information from activities like online resources, media resources, emails, newsletters etc.

Disseminator:

In disseminator role managers shares the information with their team and management by holding meetings, emails, text messages, phone calls, circulars etc.

Spokesperson:

In spokesperson role the managers communicates information on the behalf of the organization to customers and stakeholders by meeting, blogs, social media, newspaper etc.

Lack of information causes major problems in organizations as once it happened to me or might have happened to many others. As a result proficient manager must keep themselves and their team informed but make sure you only share information that you are allowed to share.

Manager is Vital Link in Gathering and Delivering Information

TELECOM CUSTOMER SERVICE STORY

This story will show that keeping yourself and your people informed is very essential. Information should involve all kind of information, specifications and company updates along with targets.

Customer Care Executive: Good Evening! XYZ Telecom, How can I help you today?

Me: Good Evening! My mobile number is 89xxx333xx. This morning I top up my mobile with INR 253 plan, that states it gives full talk time and 1GB free internet browsing but it's been more than 12 hours and every time I use internet I am being charged.

Can you please help me with this as I shouldn't be charged for browsing?

Customer Care Executive: Surely, I will help you with this Sir! Can you please confirm me your details?

Me: I am Gaurav Gulati and my mobile number is 89xxx333xx

Customer Care Executive: Thank you for confirming your details. Mr. Gulati, can I put you on hold while I check your account information?

Me: Sure, please take your time.

Customer Care Executive: Sorry for keeping you waiting, I have checked the information and I am sorry to inform you that no offer of INR 253 is running at the moment.

Me: How is this possible? I have visited your company's website and it had banner for this INR 253 plan offer. In fact I have top up by clicking the banner and then paid for it. Can you please check the website and see its still there . . .

Customer Care Executive: Please hold, I will check the information again.

Me: Ok

Customer Care Executive: You are right, the offer banner is still online but unfortunately the offer is not available on our systems, therefore you will not get 1GB free data and it shall be charged every time you browse. I am sorry for inconvenience; we will get that banner removed from website soon.

Me: It's funny, how can your company be so irresponsible? Can you please take my complaint and provide me with the complaint number?

Customer Care Executive: Sir, I ask your patience. Please be online, I will connect you to our customer satisfaction manager.

Manager: Good Evening Mr. Gulati! I am George, customer satisfaction manager. I have been informed by our executive about your complaint and I apologize for this. We shall soon get the INR 253 offer banner removed from our website. But unfortunately we can't provide you complaint number for this, I request you to please understand.

Me: Thanks for your service (And angrily I disconnected the call)

This didn't end here and I decided to visit the website and check the offer again. I visited the XYZ Telecom website and after carefully reading the offer I read that offer clearly stated; "The offer may vary in some regions please manually select your region to check offer for your region". After selecting my region manually, I noticed that for my region the offer had only full talk value and didn't have free 1 GB internet.

I realized my mistake. I didn't carefully read the offer but I was surprised to know even the customer service executive and customer satisfaction manager were not aware of the offer. This only happens when companies don't keep their employees updated or when managers don't take pains to keep themselves informed and updated.

THINK PAGE

Think and write down your plans and thoughts that you have made after reading this chapter. This "Think Page" will help you create an action plan and ideas that you can use to bring change and improvement in your life to be proficient manager.

Space above is intentionally left blank. Use blank space to write your ideas and plans

CREATIVE PROBLEM SOLVING

7

W e all are surrounded by various kinds of issues both personal and professional. Managers have so much to do; they are responsible for their employees and are always surrounded with various challenges and problems. Thus to overcome these problems it becomes mandatory for managers to develop problem solving skills.

Creative problem solving skills can be used in countless ways. People generally associate creative problem solving skills with dealing with crisis and difficulties but it is the skill that is required for achieving exceptional performance in your job. This skill will turn you more creative and innovative and will help you turn difficult challenges and transform them into opportunity.

We need to know that everyone is creative, and that everyone has its own way of contributing in creative process. Creative problem solving is different from routine problem solving as it is not pre-established method and it involves a hunt for new solution.

Creative problem solving basically can be defined as the assumption that you know something that can help you solve problems and challenges. It can also be described as an attitude that makes you believe you can resolve any problem or challenge without depending on routine pre-established methods.

The question is how managers can enhance problem solving ability? The key step to enhance problem solving ability is to think outside the box and believe every problem can be solved. The final step is vital, it is to choose among options and take action with dedication and responsibility.

TIPS FOR EFFECTIVE PROBLEM SOLVING

Accept the Problem:

The key to solving a problem is to accept them. When you accept that the problem already exists and stop resisting then you put your all energy and efforts to resolve it.

Be Clear:

This may sound so basic, but don't make assumption. Get real information to understand the problem clearly before you focus on finding the right solution. Clarity will put your efforts in the right place.

Be Optimistic:

Optimism does not mean ignoring the problem in fact it means every problem can be solved. Staying positive in hard times can be difficult but optimism can make you a better problem solver.

Set a Right Goal:

Goals matter. The right goal brings satisfaction you deserve after all the hard work. Whenever you set a goal always ask yourself what exactly you want? This will help you resolve your issue right away.

Be Open Minded:

An efficient problem solver is open-minded to other people's opinions and viewpoints. It means you are flexible and adaptive to new experiences and ideas. Open mindedness will help you in problem solving and create new opportunities for you.

Take Other People's Opinions:

You should not hesitate taking other people's opinion on what to do and what they would do in similar kind of situation. Accept the fact; "You can't solve every problem on your own".

Think Outside the Box:

Too much of logical thinking can prevent you from innovative thoughts but creative problem solving is process of generating new ideas. Sometimes, we tend to stick to pre-established methods and don't try other ways, whereas creative problem solving is only possible when you think outside the box.

THE PHILOSOPHY STUDENT AND CHAIR STORY

A philosophy professor gave an unusual test to his class. He lifted his chair onto his desk and wrote on the board simply: "Prove that this chair does not exist."

The class set to work, composing long complex explanations—except one student, who took just thirty seconds to complete and hand in his paper, attracting surprised glances from his classmates and the professor. Few days later the class received their grades for the test.

The student who took 30 seconds was judged the best. His answer was, "What Chair?"

This short story about creative problem solving teaches us that creative problem solving is all about thinking outside the box and it really doesn't matter how long you take to resolve the problem.

THINK PAGE

Think and write down your plans and thoughts that you have made after reading this chapter. This "Think Page" will help you create an action plan and ideas that you can use to bring change and improvement in your life to be proficient manager.

Space above is intentionally left blank. Use blank space to write your ideas and plans

8

END BLAME CULTURE

Every organization has to have positive culture, unfortunately many organizations are being affected by culture of blame and at such a workplace if something goes wrong people look for someone to blame.

Not accepting mistakes and blaming others is not the mindset of learner. Forwarding blames for protecting self-image can damage reputation of self and organization. Blame culture is not only blaming others but it is even worst when managers or employees take each others blame on themselves to save someone from trouble.

The organizations where blaming is the culture perform badly and are less creative, many researchers and experts believes blaming is like communicable disease and organizations must take steps to stop the culture of blame. A recent survey developed by OfficeTeam, the world's leading staffing firm shows that 30% of the managers have taken the blame at work for something that wasn't their fault.

A culture of blame shows fundamental issue with leadership. Creating and maintaining a positive, blameless and motivating culture at workplace is the responsibility of the manager. Managers must know how to handle blame culture and must do something to change culture of blame into culture of responsibility and positivity. Managers must help their people build confidence and encourage them to speak truth. They need to remind employees of past successes, not past failures.

Organization without culture of blame means successful organization. There are many ways in which managers can end blame culture and the first step to begin this is by establishing good relationships, improving teamwork and fostering innovations. This will build a positive work environment and end blame culture.

TIPS TO END BLAME CULTURE

Don't Blame Others:

Managers should set an example for their teams by not blaming anyone and should accept their mistakes. By accepting mistakes openly in front of their teams they will encourage honesty and truth.

Respect Who Accept:

Never criticize people who accept their mistakes in fact demonstrate respect for their honesty and courage. In unavoidable circumstances managers should express their aggression only for mistakes not for the honesty as it will discourage others to speak truth.

Avoid Punishments:

Avoid practice of punishment especially when someone accepts their mistake. Employees commonly blame others to protect themselves from punishments so it is good to avoid punishments.

Create Culture of Learning:

We all make mistakes and creating culture of learning from mistakes can prevent it to happen again. Managers should create learning culture where employees should feel free to talk about their mistakes and can learn from them.

Don't Laugh at Others Mistakes:

A childish practice like laughing at others mistake also becomes biggest reason for employees to blame others to hide their mistakes. We should learn from others mistakes rather than laughing on them.

Old & New Manager Story

Once upon a time in a famous company an Old Manager was to retire and a new and young one was to take charge. The retiring Manager was quiet old, qualified and well experienced.

While leaving, the retiring manager shared his experiences and achievements with the new manager. The New Manager asked the retiring manager for some expertise tips. The old retiring manager prepared two sealed envelopes for the new manager and labeled them as 'Crisis One' and 'Crisis Two'. The old manager while handing over the envelops to the new manager said; "Whenever you face a critical management crisis for the first time open the first envelope and for any other similar and further critical management crisis open the second envelope. Both these will help you in any kind of a management crisis, and trust me; this is the testimony of my decades of experience". The new manager took both envelops very happily and they both departed wishing good luck on each other's journey.

Times went on and after few years the new manager faced a bad management crisis for the first time. Sales were very poor, targets under achieved and employees were highly de-motivated. The management was very angry on the whole situation.

The young manager was in a deep trouble, for the very first time he remembered old manager and he could also recollect the two envelopes that he had given to him while departing. He opened the first envelope which was sealed and labeled as 'Crisis One'. The expertise tip that was written in the letter was, **"Blame Previous Manager"** The young manager was very happy and quickly thought of implementing it. He called his entire team, took them in confidence and shared the new winning strategy. They all started blaming the old manager and his team for all the failures. They all blamed the old manager and his team for all their planning, forecasting, strategies and leadership. The young managers saved him and his team from management crisis and got another opportunity from management.

Time passed and after few years the young manager faced another worst management crisis. Sales were very poor, targets under achieved and people were highly de-motivated. This time the management was very unhappy, angry and annoyed with the young manager and his team. This appeared to be the last chance . . . Not having any other option, young manager opened the second envelope which was sealed and labeled as 'Crisis Two'. The expertise tip written in the second letter said, **"Prepare Two Similar Envelops for the New Incoming Manager"**. You can not fool all the people all the time.

We Can Take Many Morals from This Story:

- Culture of blame is hereditary and can spread like communicable disease.
- One has to understand blaming others is never the solution and blaming others cannot protect self-image for long. Someday truth will come out.
- The organizations where blaming is the culture perform poorly and are less creative.
- Someone has to take first step to change the culture.

THINK PAGE

Think and write down your plans and thoughts that you have made after reading this chapter. This "Think Page" will help you create an action plan and ideas that you can use to bring change and improvement in your life to be proficient manager.

Space above is intentionally left blank. Use blank space to write your ideas and plans

9

BE TRUTHFUL TO YOUR CUSTOMER

B e truthful to your customers and clients because your lies may not change the company's future but surely can change yours. Employees from almost all the sectors lie to their customers and clients believing speaking truth will result revenue loss.

Why employees don't speak truth?

While working with various sectors like retail, banking and insurance both in India and United Kingdom, I learned Government and Regulatory Bodies has made it mandatory for companies to tell important information like risk level, disclaimer, terms and conditions to its customers but many employees hide or manipulates these information as most of them believe speaking all the truth will lead to loss of customer and revenue.

Keep in mind, sooner or later truth comes out. So it is suicidal to speak lies and hide facts while making promises to customers. These unethical practices may result profitable in the beginning but they are career destructing at lateral stage.

Most employees while speaking lies justify themselves by believing:

➢ Everyone does this I am not the exception.
➢ If I won't do it, I won't be able to keep my job.
➢ I am just doing it now. I will soon switch job, so it's the next manager's obligation to handle these customers and clients.

Most employees while following these beliefs forget:

➢ Employees forget that they can switch job but can't leave the world if they are found guilty. They may manage to protect themselves from judicial obligation but they can't protect their image.
➢ It is not important you have to do everything that others do. A principled person is different from others and he/ she only do things that are ethically correct.
➢ If the path of dishonesty is only way to keep your job then it is better to quit and find yourself a new job. Find a job where truth and ethics are appreciated as unethical practices will not let you live happily and peacefully.

This happens mainly due to lack of values-based training of employees. Companies often focus only on training of products, services and procedures but they forget or intentionally don't train their employees about result of hiding truth and false promises. In reality by hiding the truth and by making false promises we may make companies financially stronger but weaker ourselves.

How to change these practices?

It is duty of every manager to teach value based management to his/her people and encourage them to speak truth. Everyone needs to understand unethical practices can destroy you in long go.

Conclusion:

If truth wasn't so painful, companies would have written disclaimers, terms and conditions in bolt letters.

Many companies don't focus on values-based training because they know too much of truth will lead to loss of customer and profits.

Employees and managers have to realize that truth and ethical practices are for the benefit of everyone (you, your company and customers).

THINK PAGE

Think and write down your plans and thoughts that you have made after reading this chapter. This "Think Page" will help you create an action plan and ideas that you can use to bring change and improvement in your life to be proficient manager.

Space above is intentionally left blank. Use blank space to write your ideas and plans

TAKE CUSTOMER SERVICE AND FEEDBACK SERIOUSLY

Good customer service begins at the top. Customer service skills are the skills that every manager and employees must master, especially if they are facing the customers. Good managers recognize the value of customer feedback and know how feedback can better the customer service.

Feedback gives information that is required for sound decision-making. Indeed, it's important for managers to encourage and accept feedback from customers and employees because it helps in the improvement and alteration of services and products. Unfortunately, many managers don't realize that it is the way to improve customer service. Taking customer's word for granted is like digging company's grave.

Managers should appreciate feedback as it is the best way to understand customer needs and concerns. Sometimes the problems are created by managers which they don't realize because they don't take feedback for themselves, they believe they are the best. But feedback should not be limited to customers, products and services but like everything else, managers need to know how they are doing overall, thus should take feedback for themselves from the people they manage.

Make changes that bring improvement without destroying values. Managers should be capable of filtering feedback; they should take feedback positively but don't forget not every feedback is for positive. Act smart! Don't hesitate to ask more feedback if you are not sure of something.

Interacting with everyone will bring you both problems and solutions. Talk to your customers and team on daily basis, you will get better feedbacks by speaking and listening as comparison to what you get on feedback form. Keeping customers happy is the responsibility of the manager and only good customer service can keep the customers happy. This will increase your chance of keeping and increasing your customer base.

Instruct your people to be always helpful and courteous. Customer service can become amazing if every member of organization understands it. Even if you have training manager still personally explain and train your people about customer service, this will set priority and pressure your people to understand the value of customer service.

TIPS FOR GREAT CUSTOMER SERVICE

Start with a Smile:

Smiling immediately puts the customer at ease and shows that you are ready to help and understand. When you smile and offer a friendly greet, it will help to calm down angry customer.

Listen Carefully:

Listen carefully to what your customers are communicating to you. Be prepared to listen completely and understand what the customer wants to express. Ask for clarification, if you are unable to understand something.

Stay Calm:

Try to manage your emotions and don't act defensive. Unsatisfied customer can act very aggressive so it is important for managers to stay calm and listen carefully. When you stay calm your customer feel much more respected.

Keep Your Promises:

Most of the complaints are based on promises, this nature of complaints and anger can be the most difficult to handle. Don't tempt the customers with promises you can't keep because in business promises are to be kept.

Be Reliable & Explain the Process:

Show your customers that you are professional and capable of providing services as per their expectation. Make sure you explain your customers about your process and procedures along with time as this will avoid any nature of misunderstanding.

Apologize If Required:

You should learn to accept your mistakes but never start the conversation with apology, make sure to hear what the other person have to say. Your apology can calm down the customer and will help to retain the customer so apologize if required. There can be cases when customer might not be right but even then they should be accommodated.

Take Feedback from Customers:

It's all about feedback, isn't it? So Ask for customer feedback and learn to successfully utilize them to bring improvement and deliver great customer service. Every customer interaction is an opportunity for feedback, be courageous and talk to as many customers as you can and make sure you talk to all kind of customers. You can also use feedback forms, questionnaires or can conduct surveys to know customer feedback.

Take Feedback from Your Team:

Talk to sales team, customer care team and other people of your team for their feedback. These people get to know customers better as they directly deal with them and have more opportunity to talk to them.

Learn to Say "Yes":

You can't say yes to everything but there are many complaints and requests of the customers that doesn't make difference to organization but make big difference to the customer. So make sure that you are flexible, and if saying "yes" doesn't have any negative impact on the organization, than say "yes".

SAINSBURY'S TIGER BREAD TALE

It is the story of a three-year old little girl Lily Robinson and Sainsbury's Supermarkets Ltd, commonly known as Sainsbury's the second largest chain of supermarkets in the United Kingdom.

The story began on 31st May 2011 when three-year old Lily Robinson wrote to Sainsbury's London head office to question: Why tiger bread is called tiger bread? And it should be called giraffe bread.

The reason Lily Robinson sent a letter to Sainsbury because tiger bread had splotches which actually resembled the splotches on a giraffe. She wrote to say that it should be renamed.

We don't know what happened in the head office and what all efforts were made by Sainsbury's customer manager after reading Lily Robinson letter . . . but on 14th June 2011, the three-old Lily Robinson received the letter from customer manager, Chris King, responding to Lily that they are agreeing with her idea.

Chris King wrote "I think renaming the bread as giraffe bread is a brilliant idea—it does look more like the blotches on a giraffe than the stripes on a tiger, doesn't it?" King also enclosed £ 3 gift card for Lily to spend in the store, and buy her own tiger bread.

How did the manager response benefit the brand and what managers can learn from this?

We understand, renaming the bread may not be the sole decision of customer manager but even if it involved people at higher management, we still appreciate Sainsbury's customer manager Chris King who took initiative and forward the customer feedback to get approval to rename the bread.

This incident attracted many customers as it made strong impression of great customer service. Sainsbury's response to customer feedback bought hundreds of compliments for both Sainsbury and customer manager, Chris King.

This incident shows how managers should take feedback, especially when feedbacks are genuine and worth considering. This is the learning for all the managers who doesn't take pains of sharing customer feedback with the management and just justify customers saying such line "Sorry Sir/Madam, it is the company decision we can't help you on this."

This is also a lesson for all the organizations that doesn't believe in taking customer feedback and do as per their liking.

THINK PAGE

Think and write down your plans and thoughts that you have made after reading this chapter. This "Think Page" will help you create an action plan and ideas that you can use to bring change and improvement in your life to be proficient manager.

Space above is intentionally left blank. Use blank space to write your ideas and plans

11

SOCIAL NETWORKING

Many people and organizations love social networking and whereas some hate it. Importance of social networking should not be underestimated; statistics as on 2013 shows that there are over 1 Billion Facebook users worldwide whereas Google+ has more than 500 Million users, LinkedIn has over 220 Million users and Twitter has over 200 million users, in addition to these there are hundreds of social networking websites and apps used by millions and billions of users worldwide.

Many managers already know the importance of using social media and they understand that you can't ignore millions and billions of users. Social Networking is an opportunity for managers to connect with customers, employees, candidates and opportunities. It is the best platform to advertise and influence customer opinions. Along with this social networking helps in hiring as organizations these days are using these means to find potential employees.

Some Benefits of Social Networking:

Easy Sales:

It's a good platform to generate sales as you can easily contact as many people you want and can reach target audience. But make sure you must know where your audience is?

Example: You have cricket match tickets for sale all you have to do is just post your advertisement on cricket fan page and you will get customers easily.

Customer Service:

Just add your customers in your connections or friend list and this become easiest way to stay connected with your customers. Effortlessly you can easily post latest offers, announcements etc, this saves your time and helps you to provide customer service round the clock.

Example: Now days Information Technology companies like Dell, HP, Apple etc posts troubleshooting tips and tools on these social networking platforms to provide customer service round the clock without spending too much time and money.

Learning:

You get to learn lot as people and organizations share so much of valuable information online that is why social networking also enhance your knowledge. To make it possible make sure you follow leaders and organizations of your interest to keep yourself updated and informed.

Increase Efficiency:

As there are millions and billions of users it makes it easy to advertise, find customers, candidates, and all this for free or at very low cost and all this you can do anytime, anywhere and really fast.

If you are still not convinced with benefits of social networking and believe that it is interruption that reduce efficiency then let me update you; recent study found that use of social media increases employees productivity. The survey conducted by Microsoft Corporation has confirmed that nearly half of employees' report that social tools at workplace help increase their productivity. Many of you may think what about of remaining half? Observing so many benefits of social media we can believe that if remaining half are not benefited they are not in loss too, networking never goes waste sooner or later it is surely going to benefit them in some form.

Networking is about making connections, successful executives, managers, entrepreneurs, companies, celebrities and almost everyone have been benefited by it. So if you don't have social networking profiles then you must create one today and if you already have it then start using it smartly.

SOCIAL NETWORKING DO'S AND DON'TS

But before you get started; you must know what actually you want to attain? Find yourself the right social networking platform to have maximum benefits. Example: For advertising and customers you can use Facebook and for professional services and opportunities use LinkedIn.

Successful social networking is not just about creating your profile and adding people in your network. You must carefully follow do's and don'ts practices of social networking to make professional impression.

Do's:

- ➢ Complete your profile; make sure you have designation and experience columns filled.
- ➢ Endorse yourself by sharing your achievements.
- ➢ Share articles, video and other content that people in your contacts may find useful.
- ➢ Promote your products and services this will help you achieve your targets easily.
- ➢ Maintain your account and update it daily but make sure to understand privacy settings.
- ➢ Follow your colleagues, boss, management, customers, company, competitors and industry leaders, this will keep you updated.
- ➢ Remember to wish your friends and contacts on their birthdays, anniversaries and special occasions; this will help you preserve relations.

Don'ts:

- ➢ Don't lie particularly about your education and professional details, you will eventually get caught.

- ➢ Never share sensitive professional information like new projects, client's details etc.
- ➢ Never share too much information about your personal and professional life.
- ➢ Don't ever use abusive words, language and share anything offensive.
- ➢ Never share negative comments on your colleagues, boss and employer.
- ➢ Don't over update your profile or send too many posts.
- ➢ Avoid making unnecessary comments on other's posts and pictures.
- ➢ Respect personal and professional life of others and never enter someone's privacy by commenting and sharing their posts.
- ➢ Don't spend too less or too much time online.

Think Page

Think and write down your plans and thoughts that you have made after reading this chapter. This "Think Page" will help you create an action plan and ideas that you can use to bring change and improvement in your life to be proficient manager.

Space above is intentionally left blank. Use blank space to write your ideas and plans

12

HEALTHY LIFESTYLE AND FITNESS

Health issues remain one of the top reasons for employees to take leave from work. Workplace absenteeism becomes big problem for managers as they have many important roles to play and as a result even a single day absence creates difficulty.

Health and lifestyle issues not simply means absence but it is the big concern for self, as unhealthy lifestyle can cause diabetes, obesity and other health problems. Every one of us should have healthy lifestyle not just to have better productivity at workplace but to live life healthily.

Recent studies have shown healthy eating, workout and, productivity are all correlated. Employees with regular workout routine and good lifestyle are more energetic and productive. It means that managers should follow healthy lifestyle and must encourage their team to follow it to enhance their performance and productivity.

With busy schedules taking time for healthy lifestyle can be challenge but this can be resolved by organizing time. To develop good lifestyle one can create reminders or can use apps on their phone, these will remind them when to eat and workout on time.

TIPS FOR KEEPING YOURSELF AND YOUR EMPLOYEES FIT

Laughter:

Laughter is powerful stress-relief medicine. Studies shows laughter creates happiness, increase immunity and even reduce pain. So whenever possible try sharing jokes and Laugh Out Loud to fight stress and make life easier. A person who laughs lot has reduced levels of stress hormone and has healthy heart.

Workout:

Workout will not only help you develop muscles and lose weight, but it can improve your mood, stamina, fitness and reduce the risk of developing diseases including depression and anxiety. Many of you may think you don't have time to exercise but there are many ways to indulge yourself in physical activities like walking, jogging, dancing etc they save time as comparison to going to gym.

Healthy Eating:

A healthy eating is the basis for a well functioning body. When it comes to healthy eating it means you should eat to improve and maintain your health. One should eat meals on time and never skip meals as it can cause anxiety, acidity and can even imbalance blood sugar and blood pressure levels.

Take Small Breaks:

Take small break of few minutes every hour. This will refresh you and will increase your focus and capacity to do more work. You can do this by stretching your arms and shoulders, stand up and walk or exercise on your desk.

Sleep Properly:

We often hear "I don't sleep much because I don't waste my time sleeping" or similar kind of statements. This is not the statement of hard working person but the statement of a foolish person because sleep is essential for a well functioning body. People who don't sleep enough lack in concentration and get stressed quickly.

Routine Health Check-Ups:

Routine health check-ups are important. Getting a routine check-up is the best way to stay healthy and ahead of disease.

Wrong Sitting Posture

Correct Sitting Posture

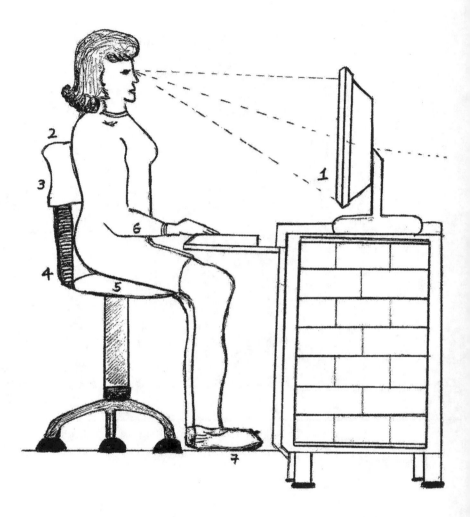

1. **Viewing Distance:** Visual Display Terminal (VDT) within the normal cone of vision
2. **Upper Back:** Keep you back straight
3. **Lower Back:** Support Lumbar Curve
4. **Hips:** Distributed Pressure
5. **Thigh Behind the Knee:** Distributed Pressure
6. **Arms:** Minimal Bend at the Wrist
7. **Feet:** Flat on Floor

Workout at Your Desk

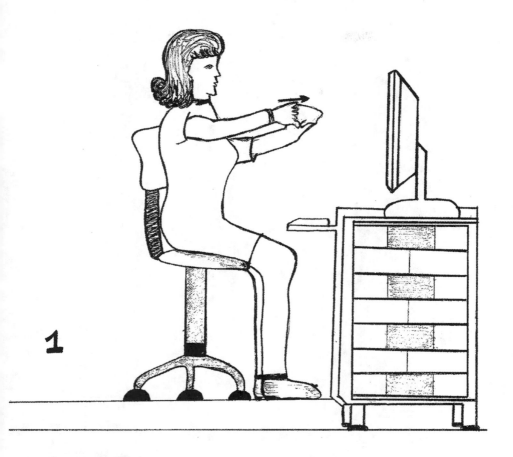

1

Hand Together, Fingers Interlaced and Extend Arms with Palms Reaching Forward

(Stretch 3 Times Minimum for 8-10 Seconds Each)

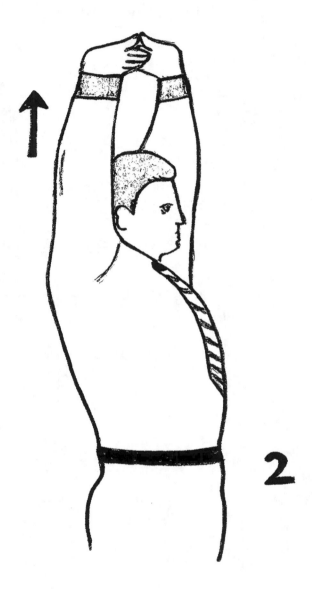

Fingers Interlaced, Move Arms Over Head with Palms Reaching Upward

(Stretch 3 Times Minimum for 8-10 Seconds Each)

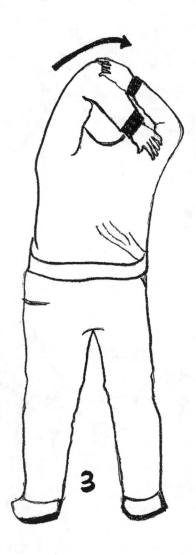

Arms Behind the Head, Grab a Hold of Opposite Elbow. Then Bend Each Side Repeatedly

(Bend 3 Times Minimum for 5-10 Seconds Each Side)

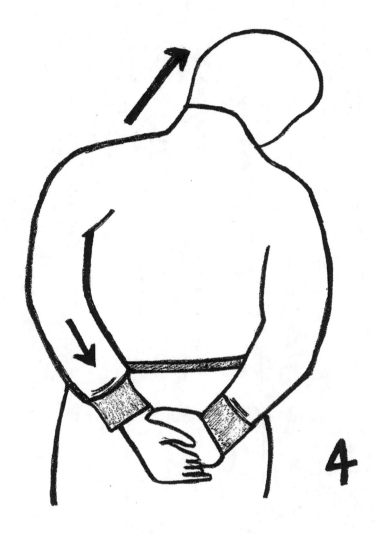

Hand Behind Hips, Bend Your Head Each Side Repeatedly

(Bend 3 Times Minimum for 5-8 Second Each Side)

Palms Together, Fingers Pointing Up, Move Hands Downward

(Stretch 3 Times Minimum for 8-12 Seconds Each)

Palms Together, Fingers Pointing Down, Move Hands Upward

(Stretch 3 Times Minimum for 8-12 Seconds Each)

Lift Your Arms Upward above Your Head, Do it with Both Arms Repeatedly

(Bend 3 Times Minimum for 5-10 Seconds Each Side)

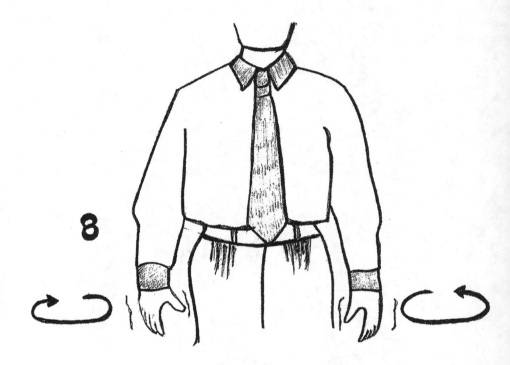

Shake Your Hands and Arms

(Do it for 3 Times for 5-10 Seconds Each Side)

Twist and Turn Both Sides

(Twist and Turn 3 Times Minimum for 5-10 Seconds Each Side)

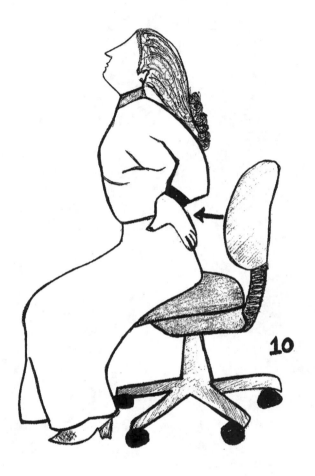

Sit Down on Chair, Place Hands on Lower Back and Stretch Yourself

(Stretch 3 Times Minimum for 5-10 Seconds Every Time)

THINK PAGE

Think and write down your plans and thoughts that you have made after reading this chapter. This "Think Page" will help you create an action plan and ideas that you can use to bring change and improvement in your life to be proficient manager.

Space above is intentionally left blank. Use blank space to write your ideas and plans

13

SOCIETAL RESPONSIBILITIES

In today's world we are all concerned about the social and environmental issues. It is the time when every one of us must act socially responsible and contribute to society and environment. Our contribution can reduce issues like corruption, racism, poverty, hunger, nature and animal conservation etc.

Societal responsibility is a duty that every person has to carry out to preserve a balance between the economy and the ecosystem. Managers should know their social responsibilities that mean they should perform their duties to contribute for welfare of the society and environment.

As an individual you should recognize your responsibility to give back to the society and environment. We are born on this common earth like everyone else, thus it is our duty to do something for the benefit of this world.

Good managers are the role model of their people and others in the organization. They are capable of influencing and encouraging their people and others to act socially responsible in a positive way, even if it's just on small scale.

Proficient manager can participate in this movement by spending just few minutes of their by discussing issues with their customers, team and others in organization with intention of providing solutions to others how everyone can participate for welfare of society and environment. But before you promote these initiatives it is important you participate yourself in them in some way so that you can set an example for others.

Everyone can bring changes by contributing little by joining communities, organizations and initiatives that focus on specific issues and concerns; there are many organizations worldwide which work actively and doing really well to bring changes in society and environment.

The Earth Charter Initiative

The Earth Charter is a declaration of fundamental ethical principles for building a just, sustainable and peaceful global society in the 21st century. It seeks to inspire in all people a new sense of global interdependence and shared responsibility for the well-being of the whole human family, the greater community of life, and future generations. It is a vision of hope and a call to action.

The Earth Charter is centrally concerned with the transition to sustainable ways of living and sustainable human development. Ecological integrity is one major theme. However, the Earth Charter recognizes that the goals of ecological protection, the eradication of poverty, equitable economic development, respect for human rights, democracy, and peace are interdependent and indivisible. It provides, therefore, a new, inclusive, integrated ethical framework to guide the transition to a sustainable future.

To find ways to Get Involved with The Earth Charter visit The Earth Charter Initiative official website for more information: http://www.earthcharterinaction.org/

Hope for Children

Hope for Children (HOPE) is a UK based charity which works towards a world where children's rights are realised and they can reach their full potential. They actively identify disadvantaged children and communities by working with local partners.

Through empowering, collaborating and learning together they aim to build a sustainable future for the children and communities they serve. There focus is to reach as many children as they can and deliver to them the childhood every child deserves.

To find ways to support Hope for Children and help children visit Hope for Children official website for more information: http://www.hope-for-children.org/

PETA

People for the Ethical Treatment of Animals (PETA) is the largest animal rights organization in the world, with more than 3 million members and supporters.

PETA focuses its attention on the four areas in which the largest numbers of animals suffer the most intensely for the longest periods of time: on factory farms, in the clothing trade, in laboratories, and in the entertainment industry. They work on a variety of other issues, including the cruel killing of beavers, birds, and other "pets" as well as cruelty to domesticated animals. PETA works through public education, cruelty investigations, research, animal rescue, legislation, special events, celebrity involvement, and protest campaigns.

To find ways to support PETA and help animals visit PETA official website for more information: http://www.peta.org

The Nature Conservancy

The Nature Conservancy is the leading conservation organization working around the world to protect ecologically important lands and waters for nature and people.

To find ways to support The Nature Conservancy visit their official website for more information: http://www.nature.org/

There are many more organizations all around the world working dedicatedly for welfare of society and environment. So find out the organization in your area or online or choose one from above to contribute your support and participate to make a change.

THINK PAGE

Think and write down your plans and thoughts that you have made after reading this chapter. This "Think Page" will help you create an action plan and ideas that you can use to bring change and improvement in your life to be proficient manager.

Space above is intentionally left blank. Use blank space to write your ideas and plans

QUOTES AND SAYINGS
FOR PROFICIENT MANAGERS

"Accept Change it may bring improvement."

"If Trust is Gone, Interest is Gone and If Face Value is Gone, Communication is Gone"

"It is important to accept as only acceptance can bring change."

"It is not important what you say but it is important how you say."

"It is not just others who make you angry and mad, you yourself do that sometimes."

"Patience is the secret of success and resolution of any problem."

"Proficient Managers Empower People to Achieve Their Goals."

"Respect who Accept"

"Say Yes to Networking, Yes to invitations, even if it's not understandable what you get out of them? Life is fickle . . . you never know they may benefit you."

"To every statement there should be justification or else it make no sense."

CONCLUSION

If you've made this far I believe that some of what you've read has proved motivating and will be useful to you both in your professional and personal life.

This book has been about practicalities of handling managerial position, and has focused on skills, abilities and behavior that are important to be proficient manager of 21st century who is capable of managing people and work smoothly.

I sincerely hope by now you've, or will become 21st century proficient manager.

Best wishes and good luck!

Gaurav Gulati

BIBLIOGRAPHY

Concise Oxford English Dictionary. 2007. 11th ed. United Kingdom: OXFORD University Press.

Employees' health and safety responsibilities | indirect. 2013. *Employees' health and safety responsibilities | indirect.* [ONLINE] Available at: http://www.nidirect.gov.uk/employees-health-and-safety-responsibilities [Accessed 02 November 2013].

Facebook's 10th birthday: from college dorm to 1.23 billion users | Technology | The Guardian. 2014. *Facebook's 10th birthday: from college dorm to 1.23 billion users | Technology | The Guardian.* [ONLINE] Available at: http://www.theguardian.com/technology/2014/feb/04/facebook-10-years-mark-zuckerberg

[Accessed 05 Feb 2014]

G.Bennis, Warren, 2009. On Becoming a Leader, Twentieth Anniversary Edition. United States of America: Perseus Books Group.

Jack Daniel's Tennessee Whiskey.2013. *Jack Daniels Tennessee Whiskey* [ONLINE] Available at: http://www2.jackdaniels.com/JackDaniel/ [Accessed 30 October 2013].

Kelly Services. 2013. *Employers Have a Direct Impact on Employee Job Satisfaction According to Global Survey by Kelly Services(R).* [ONLINE] Available at: http://ir.kellyservices.com/releasedetail.cfm?ReleaseID=791220. [Accessed 09 October 2013].

Kotter, John P., 2001. What Leaders Really Do. *What Leaders Really Do. BEST OF HBR.* [Online]. DECEMBER 2001, 3. Available at: http://inet.katz.pitt.edu/studentnet/projects/ceestaging/upmc2012/What%20Leaders%20Really%20Do.pdf [Accessed on 11 November 2013].

Microsoft. 2011. *Connect with Customers Through Social Media.* [ONLINE] Available at: http://www.microsoft.com/enterprise/nl-be/it-trends/social-enterprise/articles/Connect-with-Customers-Through-Social-Media.aspx#fbid=yfP12li-pAE. [Accessed 15 January 14].

Mind Tools. 2013.*Henri Fayol's Principles of Management* [ONLINE] Available at: http://www.mindtools.com/pages/article/henri-fayol.htm [Accessed 20 October 2013.]

Number of active users at Facebook over the years—Yahoo News.2013. *Number of active users at Facebook over the years—Yahoo News.* [ONLINE] Available at: http://news.yahoo.com/number-active-users-facebook-over-230449748.html. [Accessed 06 November 2013].

OfficeTeam.2013. *Survey: Three in 10 Executives Have Taken the Blame at Work for Something They Didn't Do.* [ONLINE] Available at: http://officeteam.rhi.mediaroom.com/blamegame. [Accessed 05 November 2013].

Seligman, Martin E.P., 2002. *Authentic Happiness.* New York, America: The Free Press

The Telegraph. 2013. *Twitter in numbers—Telegraph.* [ONLINE] Available at: http://www.telegraph.co.uk/technology/twitter/9945505/Twitter-in-numbers.html [Accessed 08 January 14].

Tennessee history, preservation and educational artifacts.2013. *Tennessee history, preservation and educational artifacts.* [ONLINE]Available at: http://www.tennesseehistory.com/class/JD.htm [Accessed 29 October 2013].